D0471472

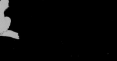

Face-to-Face
with
The Ladybug

Valérie Tracqui

Photos by Patrick Lorne

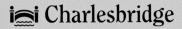 Charlesbridge

2

Ladybugs are smaller than a thumbnail.
(Shown here larger than actual size.)

Springtime

Spring begins in March. As the earth warms up, gardens burst into color. Bees slurp nectar from flowers and birds sing. Still numb from the winter cold, tiny ladybugs fly down from the mountains into the open country. One lands . . . on someone's finger. The ladybug warms itself in the sun.

Ladybugs live where they can find food. You might see ladybugs in gardens, meadows, and fields.

3

Identification

The ladybug's black-spotted red back makes it easy to identify. Each type, or species, of ladybug has a different color or number of spots.

 Ladybugs use their clawed feet to climb and their antennae to smell.

These two ladybugs are different species. The smaller ladybug lives in low-lying plants and bushes. The larger ladybug lives in trees.

🐞 *Scientists have discovered over four hundred fifty species of ladybug in North America. There are about one hundred fifty known species in the United States.*

With its round top and flat underside, ladybugs look like half a small pea. Ladybugs climb plants searching for their favorite food: aphids.

🐞 *It is not easy to see the ladybug's black compound eyes between the white spots on its head.*

Fly away

At the top of the flower, the ladybug flexes its muscles a few times to get ready to fly.

Then its wing cases open in the middle to reveal two long wings folded like fans. These wing cases are called elytra. A second later, the ladybug takes to the air.

"Ladybug, ladybug, fly away home."

 Ladybugs need warm weather to fly. People predict that summer is near when they see ladybugs in flight.

 *The ladybug's wings are twice as long as its body, so the ladybug keeps them tucked under its elytra.*

A ladybug beats its wings ninety times per second. It can fly up to thirty miles without stopping.

Ladybugs eat aphids, but ants try to protect the aphids. Aphids produce a syrup that ants eat.

At war with ants

A ladybug searches for nice, juicy aphids. Aphids feed on plants. The ladybug lands on plants to eat aphids. Ants are guarding the aphids for the syrup they produce. They bite the ladybug and force it away. The ladybug falls to the grass and plays dead for a moment. When the danger has passed, it flies away.

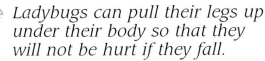 *Ladybugs can pull their legs up under their body so that they will not be hurt if they fall.*

9

What a monster!

A ladybug lands on a rose where hundreds of aphids suck the sap from the stem. The ladybug grabs a green aphid and injects a little saliva into the aphid to soften it. Mushy aphids are easier to chew. The ladybug gobbles up aphids like a monster. When the ladybug is full, it flies off to find a mate.

When a ladybug is far away, it tracks aphids by their smell. Once the ladybug gets closer, it uses its eyes to find a tasty treat.

 *A ladybug grabs its prey with its strong mandibles, or jaws, and sucks out the aphid's insides. The aphid's body deflates.*

 *In the spring, a ladybug eats up to one hundred aphids a day. During the summer, it feeds on caterpillars, plant nectar, or mushroom spores.*

 *Ladybugs mate in April.*

 The male mates with several females to fertilize their eggs.

  The ladybug lays its eggs one by one. They look like tiny yellow bowling pins lined up in groups of about fifty.

After five days, the eggs turn gray, crack open, and release little larvae.

Look out! This ladybug was busy laying her eggs, and she didn't see the spider that wanted to eat her.

Birth

The female finds a place where there is a lot of food nearby. She waits for warm weather and long days filled with sunlight. The female then lays her eggs on a leaf close to an aphid colony.

Once the larvae begin to hatch, the ladybug flies away to find a suitable place to lay her next cluster of eggs. She will lay several clusters of eggs during the next month or two.

13

Dinnertime

Only moments after its birth, the little larva begins to hunt. It stuffs itself with aphids and grows quickly. After a few days, the larva is too big for its black skin. The larva sheds.

The skin splits and the larva crawls out and expands. Its warts and hair make it look ugly. The larva is still growing, so it needs to eat more and more each day.

 *The tiny, black larva sheds its skin four times in twenty days and grows to twelve times its original size.*

 When it is one month old, the larva is nearly an inch long. It is bigger now than it will be when it becomes an adult ladybug.

 The larva eats between one hundred and one hundred fifty aphids a day.

 The larva is almost blind. It finds its prey mainly by smell.

It's a miracle!

After three weeks, the larva has grown very big. One day, it stops eating and sits still on a leaf. . . .

▲  *The larva sticks the tip of its abdomen to a leaf with a kind of glue.*

▲ *The larva sheds its skin to reveal the stiff, dry chrysalis, its protective covering.*

▲ *After ten days, the nymph begins to move, and the chrysalis tears away. A nymph is an insect that has not fully matured.*

A brand-new ladybug escapes from its old skin. It is spotless and yellow. At first its elytra are soft, dull, and dimpled like the skin of an orange. ▼

▲ *The ladybug crawls out headfirst, then turns to dry in the sun. Little by little, its elytra harden and begin to shine.*

The old, empty skin is left behind on the leaf. The ladybug opens its wings to dry them before starting its new life. ▶

Presto!

Like magic, black spots appear on the ladybug's back, and its elytra turn red. The ladybug is already hungry and begins to feast on aphids. There's no time to lose.

These black spots are just beginning to show.

This ladybug is orange when it emerges from its nymph stage, but it turns red a few hours later.

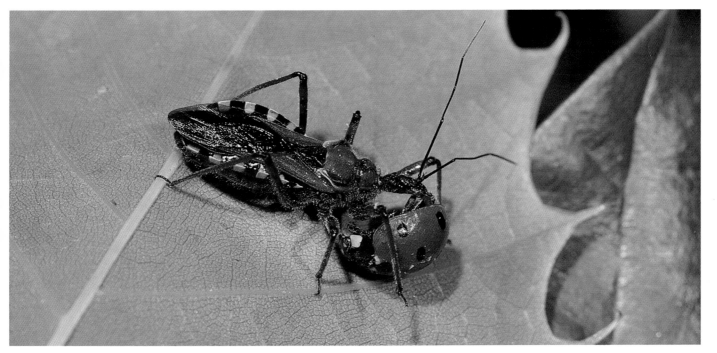

🐞 *The assassin bug is the ladybug's enemy, as are the praying mantis, the woodpecker, and many small rodents.*

🐞 *The ladybug defends itself with a bitter, smelly substance hidden in its feet.*

An assassin bug grabs the ladybug before it can release the fluid that makes it taste bad. Most animals know to avoid red insects. Many poisonous insects have an unusual color or odor to warn predators to stay away.

Ladybugs migrate to higher altitudes at the end of the summer.

Ladybugs can catch diseases when they gather in big groups.

In the winter, each species of ladybug gathers in large groups of between ten and one hundred bugs.

Brr, it's winter!

Aphids disappear when the weather turns cold, but ladybugs build up enough fat and sugar to survive without eating for five months. They settle with other ladybugs into a crack in a rock, the eaves under a roof, or some other hiding place that will be safe from the frost. Ladybugs that survive the winter wait for the first warmth of spring before they eat again.

Hurrah for ladybugs!

Everyone loves these little red bugs that signal the start of warmer weather. Ladybugs are fierce predators, and some people raise them to help get rid of aphids. Be careful not to spray ladybugs with insecticide.

Lucky charms

While many people are afraid of spiders and cockroaches, no one minds when a ladybug crawls up their finger. Ladybugs are considered lucky. Many people wear ladybug pins or necklaces as charms.

 The multicolored Asian lady beetle does not sleep as long in the winter as other species.

nature's insecticide

In the United States, people are raising various species of ladybug. The idea is for ladybugs to be placed in gardens and crops to eat other insects before these insects can damage plants. The ladybugs could replace chemical insecticides that are dangerous for all insects, humans, and the environment.

People are looking for planet-friendly ways to rid their gardens of aphids, a common garden pest.

Mail-order bugs

Since 1994, researchers at the National Agricultural Research Institute in Antibes, France, have raised a species of ladybug originally from China. This species is marketed by the Biotop society. Anyone can call a local garden center and order the greedy larva of this Asian lady beetle. The larva will be sent in the mail.

In a scientific test, ladybugs feed on aphids that are infesting these bean plants.

stag beetle

Other coleoptera

Ladybugs belong to the Coleoptera order, a group made up of hundreds of families. Each has a pair of hard wing cases, or elytra, that form a protective shell. Like the ladybug, many coleoptera eat meat, but they are not all welcomed by gardeners. . . .

Sometimes called "pinching bugs," **stag beetles** are noted for their large mandibles. The stag beetle eats sap from broken branches of trees.

Checkered beetles are red like ladybugs: a warning that keeps other animals from trying to eat them. These beetles also rid gardens of unwanted pests. Checkered beetles eat flower pollen and small insects. Their larvae feast on the larvae of solitary bees.

checkered beetle

june bug

June bugs fly at twilight. They feed on young tree leaves. Farmers and gardeners do not like their big, white larvae because they devour plant roots. Adult june bugs crawl out of the ground when they are four years old. June bugs have become rare.

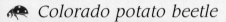

Colorado potato beetle

Colorado potato beetles attack potato plants. The female lays her eggs on the potato leaves, and then the larvae feed on the leaves.

These **ground beetles** have shiny, metallic-looking shells. They capture other insects, worms, or small snails. Some ground beetles can fly. Others move quickly on the ground. Like ladybugs, certain species of ground beetles prey on plant-eating pests.

ground beetle

25

A Quick Quiz about Ladybugs:

Photograph credits:
All photographs taken by Patrick Lorne, except:
C. Ratier: p. 8; B. Baranger: pp. 14 (bottom), 23 (bottom right); R. Konic/Jacana: p. 20 (bottom left); P. Pilloud/Jacana pp. 20-21.

Special thanks to André Ferrand and Alexandre Lavagne from the National Agricultural Research Institute in Antibes for their scientific review.